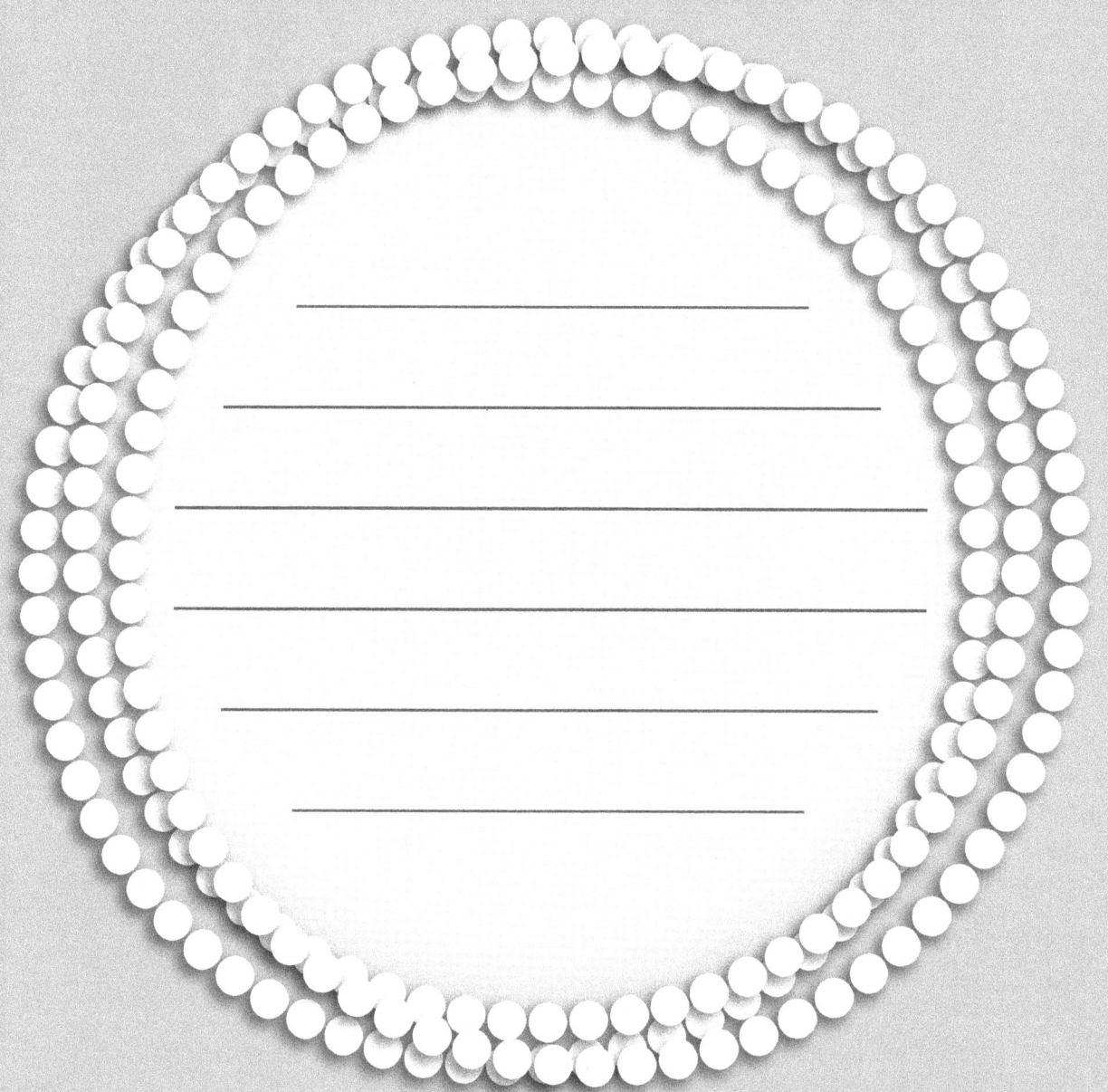

Copyright © 2020 by Annette Bridges
www.annettebridges.com

Published by Ranch House Press

All rights reserved. Except as permitted under the U.S. Copyright Act of 1976, no part of this publication may be reproduced, distributed, or transmitted in any form or by any means, or stored in a database or retrieval system, without the prior written permission of the author.

Illustrated by Lesley Vernon
www.lvdesignhouse.com

Layout and Cover Design by Janie Owen-Bugh
www.janieowenbugh.com

Printed in the United States of America.

ISBN 978-1-946371-47-8

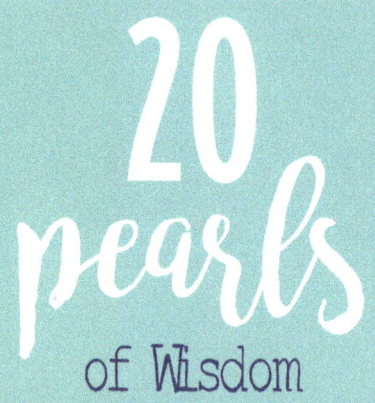

20 pearls
of Wisdom

1. Ask yourself: "but what if you could?"

2. LOVE the HELL out of 'em! (In other words...Love anyway! No matter what...In spite of...Even if you don't want to.)

3. Whatever makes your soul smile, DO THAT!

4. Find YOUR beach.

5. Your world isn't supposed to be lived in black and white. Add lots of color!

6. Be thankful for what you've got and you'll have ENOUGH to be thankful for.

7. Happiness is found by loving the life you live.

8. Don't forget to have fun!

9. Life is meant for good friends and great adventures.
10. Everything you do doesn't have to be planned. Just GO!
11. You're never too old to try something you've never done before.
12. Yes! You CAN! You always have a choice!
13. Follow your heart.
14. Be unapologetically YOU!
15. Move your body any and every way that you can.
16. Stop fretting over what's not important. GOOD ENOUGH is perfectly fine.
17. Don't let anything or anyone take your joy from you EVER!
18. Do what you CAN do!
19. Never give up!
20. You're never alone, honey!

a note from THE AUTHOR

Mamma Said So holds the words that whisper into my heart when I long to hear my mamma's voice. I present them to you so they can whisper into your heart, too. Hopefully, these messages will become what we tell ourselves because, my friends, it is what we say to our self that has the greatest power.

When I think about what Mamma said to me again and again during the sixty years we had together, I also remember how she looked into my eyes and how I felt like she was speaking into my soul. She wanted me to feel the love that impelled her every word. And I did.

Mamma made me believe anything really was possible, that I really was beautiful, that I really could do whatever I wanted to do, and that my dreams really could come true.

Her words and intentions were not warnings and admonitions. Indeed not. The world I shared with my mamma was filled with affirmations — YES, DO IT, YOU CAN, YOU'VE GOT THIS. She was very convincing!

Mamma Said So is written so I never forget her words. It's for those moments when I need encouragement and wish I could get her magnanimous hug. They are shared in bright bold colors because my mamma was bold, bright and brave and it simply felt necessary and important to display her messages and illustrate her life in as many colors as possible.

Mamma was generous with sharing her love and life with others and so I share her truths with you. These truths were well lived throughout her ninety-two years. She put them into practice in her own life. And they have left indelible imprints on my heart.

As you turn each page, I want you to pause and ponder every word and phrase. I want you to know that every truth in this book is applicable in your own life. I want you to feel the power of affirming each statement as a fact for your own life. And I want you to believe and trust the advice and promises.

Why should you know, feel, believe and trust what my mamma said as truths that are relevant to you right now at this season in your life? Because they are, my friends!
Because my mamma said so!

To everyone who knew my mamma as well as those who didn't…

May mamma's words and example remind you to make the most of your life and assure you it's never too late to do so.

ASK yourself: "BUT what IF YOU could?"

LOVE the HELL out of 'EM!

(in OTHER words... LOVE anyway!... no matter WHAT... in SPITE of... even IF you don't WANT to.)

whatever **MAKES** *your* **SOUL** *smile,* **DO THAT!**

find YOUR beach

YOUR world isn't SUPPOSED to be LIVED in BLACK and WHITE.

ADD lots of COLOR!

HAPPINESS *is* FOUND *by* LOVING *the* LIFE *you* LIVE

LIFE is meant for GOOD friends and GREAT adventures

EVERYTHING *you* DO *does*

FOLLOW *your* HEART

BE *unapologetically* YOU

MOVE *your* BODY ANY *and* EVERY *way* THAT *you* CAN

YOU'RE *never* **TOO OLD** *to try something* you've **NEVER DONE** *before*

DO what you CAN do!

about THE AUTHOR

Annette Bridges and her husband are cattle ranchers in Texas. She also writes a monthly column for North Texas Farm & Ranch magazine titled "When a city girl goes country." And she's the owner of Ranch House Gift Shop.

Annette is the author of a few books and has published other items in print such as journals, coloring books and a children's cookbook, too. She loves to paint and dream up all kinds of creations that you'll see in her gift shop.

The baby of her mamma's four children, Annette was the only girl. She began "Mamma Said So" shortly after her mamma passed in 2018. Annette wanted this book to be as bold and colorful as her mamma lived her entire life.

You can learn more about Annette at her website:
www.annettebridges.com

Shop in her Etsy Store at www.Etsy.com/shop/RanchHouseGiftShop

And follow Annette's Facebook page if you love cows, need some inspiration or giggles and want to keep up with her latest news and adventures.
www.Facebook.com/TexasAuthorAnnetteBridges

about THE ILLUSTRATOR

Lesley Vernon is an illustrator, graphic designer and fine artist. She has a BA in Fine Arts and is currently pursuing a Master's degree in Art Therapy. She has illustrated several children's coloring books and a number of other book designs with Annette Bridges. In addition, Lesley loves drawing in pen & ink and painting in watercolors.

Lesley, along with her husband and two sons, lives in southeastern Massachusetts. She spends her free time hiking in the woods and mountains of New England, practicing yoga and raising a flock of backyard chickens. She and her family enjoy being outdoors in all seasons — snowshoeing and skiing in the winter and camping together in the summer. There are so many beautiful, natural places to explore!

To find out more about Lesley's work, please visit her website at:

www.lvdesignhouse.com

about THE LAYOUT DESIGNER

A recent graduate of the Art Institute of Dallas, **Janie Owen-Bugh's** career actually started several decades ago. She's made a name for herself with her attention to detail, out-of-the-box ideas, technical savvy, and problem solving ability.

Throughout her career, she has designed numerous print and digital materials, as well as video editing for a variety of industries.

Having developed a love for publishing, in recent years she has designed dozens of books and over 50 book covers.

She lives in a suburb of Dallas, TX and enjoys spending time with her two granddaughters, painting, singing, and traveling.

To see more of Janie's work, please visit her website at:

janieowenbugh.com

(Illustrations on this page are by Janie Owen-Bugh.)

other titles by ANNETTE BRIDGES

Color-N-Doodle Your World
An inspiring collection of coloring pages with your own space to doodle and create.

My Furry Friend
A keepsake journal.

A Dachshund Tale
Lessons learned from my dog.

Color Your World Journal Series
18 themed journals.

Jot Journals
18 themed pocket-sized journals.

Oh, How the Years Fly By!
A whimsical adult coloring book.

Oh, How the Years Fly By!
A whimsical inspirational quote book.

The Gospel According to Mamma
One mother's philosophy on love, God, money, aging, decisions, change, and much more.

Be Queen of Your Life
A savvy mom helps daughters command and rule their lives.

Have Lipstick, Will Travel
How to reimagine your life, purpose, and haircolor.

Lady and Bella: Totally Different, Totally Friends
A coloring storybook for children.

Lady and Bella: Totally Friends Journal
Especially for children.

Lady and Bella's Alphabet Kitchen
A to Z recipes for kid cooks.

www.ingramcontent.com/pod-product-compliance
Lightning Source LLC
Chambersburg PA
CBHW042354280426
43661CB00095B/1044